Liberty
&Property

Liberty & Property

by
Ludwig von Mises

MISES INSTITUTE

Ludwig von Mises Institute
518 West Magnolia Avenue
Auburn, Alabama 36832
www.mises.org

ISBN: 978-1-933550-54-1

...the policies of individualism and of capitalism, its application to economic matters, do not need any apologists or propagandists. The achievements speak for themselves.

— Ludwig von Mises

C O N T E N T S

"At the end of the eighteenth century there prevailed two notions of liberty, each of them very different from what we have in mind today referring to liberty and freedom."

"The pre-capitalistic system of product was restrictive. Its historical basis was military conquest."

"What vitiates entirely the socialists' economic critique of capitalism is their failure to grasp the sovereignty of the consumers in the market economy."

"It was different in the esoteric discussions among the inner circles of the great conspiracy. There the initiated did not dissemble their intentions concerning liberty."

"Romantic philosophy labored under the illusion that in the early ages of history the individual was free and that the course of historical evolution deprived him of his primordial liberty."

"However, one does not exhaustively describe the sweeping changes that capitalism brought about in the conditions of the common man if one merely deals with the supremacy he enjoys on the market as a consumer."

"The distinctive principle of Western social philosophy is individualism. It aims at the creation of a sphere in which the individual is free to think, to choose, and to act without being restrained by the interference of the social apparatus of coercion and oppression, the State."

Liberty & Property

I

AT THE END of the eighteenth century there prevailed two notions of liberty, each of them very different from what we have in mind today referring to liberty and freedom.

The first of these conceptions was purely academic and without any application to the conduct of political affairs. It was an idea derived from the books of the ancient authors, the study of which was then the

This article was originally delivered as a lecture at Princeton University, October 1958, at the 9th Meeting of the Mont Pelerin Society.

11

sum and substance of higher education. In
the eyes of these Greek and Roman writers,
freedom was not something that had to be
granted to all men. It was a privilege of the
minority, to be withheld from the majority.
What the Greeks called democracy was, in
the light of present-day terminology, not
what Lincoln called government by the people, but oligarchy, the sovereignty of full-
right citizens in a community in which the
masses were meteques or slaves. Even this
rather limited freedom after the fourth century before Christ was not dealt with by the
philosophers, historians, and orators as a
practical constitutional institution. As they
saw it, it was a feature of the past irretriev-
ably lost. They bemoaned the passing of
this golden age, but they did not know any
method of returning to it.

The second notion of liberty was no less
oligarchic, although it was not inspired by
any literary reminiscences. It was the ambi-
tion of the landed aristocracy, and some-
times also of urban patricians, to preserve

their privileges against the rising power of royal absolutism. In most parts of continental Europe, the princes remained victorious in these conflicts. Only in England and in the Netherlands did the gentry and the urban patricians succeed in defeating the dynasties. But what they won was not freedom for all, but only freedom for an elite, for a minority of the people.

We must not condemn as hypocrites the men who in those ages praised liberty, while they preserved the legal disabilities of the many, even serfdom and slavery. They were faced with a problem which they did not know how to solve satisfactorily. The traditional system of production was too narrow for a continually rising population. The number of people for whom there was, in a full sense of the term, no room left by the pre-capitalistic methods of agriculture and artisanship was increasing. These supernumeraries were starving paupers. They were a menace to the preservation of the existing order of society and, for a long time, nobody could think of another order, a state of affairs, that would feed all of these poor wretches. There could not be any question of granting them full civil rights, still less of giving them a share of the conduct of affairs of state. The only expedient the rulers knew was to keep them quiet by resorting to force.

II

THE PRE-CAPITALISTIC system of product was restrictive. Its historical basis was military conquest. The victorious kings had given the land to their paladins. These aristocrats were lords in the literal meaning of the word, as they did not depend on the patronage of consumers buying or abstaining from buying on a market. On the other hand, they themselves were the main customers of the processing industries which, under the guild system, were organized on a corporative scheme. This scheme was opposed to innovation. It forbade deviation from the traditional methods of production. The number of people for whom there were jobs even in agriculture or in the arts and crafts was limited. Under these conditions, many a man, to use the words of Malthus, had to discover that "at nature's mighty feast there is no vacant cover for him" and that "she tells him to be gone."[1] But some of these outcasts nevertheless managed to survive, begot children, and made the number of destitute grow hopelessly more and more.

But then came capitalism. It is customary to see the radical innovations that capitalism brought about in the substitution of the mechanical factory for the more primitive and less efficient methods of the artisans' shops. This is a rather superficial view. The characteristic feature of capitalism that distinguishes it from pre-capitalist methods of production was its new principle of marketing. Capitalism is not simply mass production, but mass production to satisfy the needs of the masses. The arts and crafts of the good old days had catered almost exclusively to the wants of the well-to-do. But

---

[1] Thomas R. Malthus, *An Essay on the Principle of Population*, 2nd ed. (London, 1803), p. 531.

the factories produced cheap goods for the many. All the early factories turned out was designed to serve the masses, the same strata that worked in the factories. They served them either by supplying them directly or indirectly by exporting and thus providing for them foreign food and raw materials. This principle of marketing was the signature of early capitalism as it is of present-day capitalism. The employees themselves are the customers consuming the much greater part of all goods produced. They are the sovereign customers who are "always right." Their buying or abstention from buying determines what has to be produced, in what quantity, and of what quality. In buying what suits them best they make some enterprises profit and expand and make other enterprises lose money and shrink. Thereby they are continually shifting control of the factors of production into the hands of those businessmen who are most successful in filling their wants. Under capitalism private property of the factors of production is a social function. The entrepreneurs, capitalists, and land owners are mandataries, as it were, of the consumers, and their mandate is revocable. In order to be rich, it is not sufficient to have once saved and accumulated capital. It is necessary to invest it again and again in those lines in which it best fills the wants of the consumers. The market process is a daily repeated plebiscite, and it ejects inevitably from the ranks of profitable people those who do not employ their property according to the orders given by the public. But business, the target of fanatical hatred on the part of all contemporary governments and self-styled intellectuals, acquires and preserves bigness only because it works for the masses. The plants that cater to the luxuries of the few never attain big size. The shortcoming of nineteenth-century historians and politicians was that they failed to realize that the workers were the main consumers of the products of industry. In their view, the wage earner was a man toiling for the sole benefit of a parasitic leisure class. They labored under the delusion that the factories had impaired the lot of the manual workers. If they had paid any attention to statistics they would easily have discovered the fallaciousness of their opinion. Infant mortality dropped, the average length of life was prolonged, the population multiplied, and the average common man enjoyed amenities of which even the well-to-do of earlier ages did not dream.

However this unprecedented enrichment of the masses were merely a by-product of the Industrial Revolution. Its main achievement was the transfer of economic supremacy from the owners of land to the totality of the population. The common man was no longer a drudge who had to be satisfied with the crumbs that fell from the tables of the rich. The three pariah castes which were characteristic of the pre-capitalistic ages—the slaves, the serfs, and those people whom patristic and scholastic authors as well as British legislation from the sixteenth to the nineteenth centuries referred to as the poor—disappeared. Their scions became, in this new setting of business, not only free workers, but also customers. This radical change was reflected in the emphasis laid by business on markets. What business needs first of all is markets and again markets. This was the watch-word of capitalistic enterprise. Markets, that means patrons, buyers, consumers. There is under capitalism one way to wealth: to serve the consumers better and cheaper than other people do.

Within the shop and factory the owner—or in the corporations, the representative of the shareholders, the president—is the boss. But this mastership is merely apparent and conditional. It is subject to the supremacy of the consumers. The consumer is king, is the real boss, and the manufacturer is done for if he does not outstrip his competitors in best serving consumers.

It was this great economic transformation that changed the face of the world. It very soon transferred political power from the hands of a privileged minority into the hands of the people. Adult franchise followed in the wake of industrial enfranchisement. The common man, to whom the market process had given the power to choose the entrepreneur and capitalists, acquired the analogous power in the field of government. He became a voter.

It has been observed by eminent economists, I think first by the late Frank A. Fetter, that the market is a democracy in which every penny gives a right to vote. It would be more correct to say that representative government by the people is an attempt to arrange constitutional affairs according to the model of the market, but this design can never be fully achieved. In the political field it is always the will of the majority that prevails, and the minorities must yield to it. It serves also minorities, provided they are not so insignificant in number as to become negligible. The garment industry produces clothes not only for normal people, but also for the stout, and the publishing trade publishes not only westerns and detective stories for the crowd, but also books for discriminating readers. There is a second important difference. In the political sphere, there is no means for an individual or a small group of individuals to disobey the will of the majority. But in the intellectual field private property makes rebellion possible. The rebel has to pay a price for his independence; there are in this universe no prizes that can be won without sacrifices. But if a man is willing to pay the price, he is free to deviate from the ruling orthodoxy or neo-orthodoxy. What would conditions have been in the socialist commonwealth for heretics like Kierkegaard, Schopenauer, Veblen, or Freud? For Monet, Courbet, Walt Whitman, Rilke, or Kafka? In all ages, pioneers of new ways of thinking and acting could work only because private property made contempt of the majority's ways possible. Only a few of these separatists were themselves economically independent enough to defy the government into the opinions of the majority. But they found in the climate of the free economy among the public people prepared to aid and support them. What would Marx have done without his patron, the manufacturer Friedrich Engels?

III

WHAT VITIATES entirely the socialists' economic critique of capitalism is their failure to grasp the sovereignty of the consumers in the market economy. They see only hierarchical organization of the various enterprises and plans, and are at a loss to realize that the profit system forces business to serve the consumers. In their dealings with their employers, the unions proceed as if only malice and greed were to prevent what they call management from paying higher wage rates. Their shortsightedness does not see anything beyond the doors of the factory. They and their henchmen talk about the concentration of economic power, and do not realize that economic power is ultimately vested in the hands of the buying public of which the employees themselves form the immense majority. Their inability to comprehend things as they are is reflected in such inappropriate metaphors as industrial kingdom and dukedoms. They are too dull to see the difference between a sovereign king or duke who could be dispossessed only by a more powerful conqueror and a "chocolate king" who forfeits his "kingdom" as soon as the customers prefer to patronize another supplier. This distortion is at the bottom of all socialist plans. If any of the socialist chiefs had tried to earn his living by selling hot dogs, he would have learned something about the sovereignty of the customers. But they were professional revolutionaries and their only job was to kindle civil war. Lenin's ideal was to build a nation's production effort according to the model of the post office, an outfit that does not depend on the consumers, because its deficits are covered by compulsory collection of taxes. "The whole of society," he said, was to "become one office and one factory."[2]

---

[2] V.I. Lenin, *State and Revolution* (New York: International Publishers, s.d.) p. 84.

He did not see that the very character of the
office and the factory is entirely changed
when it is alone in the world and no longer
grants to people the opportunity to choose
among the products and services of various
enterprises. Because his blindness made it
impossible for him to see the role the market
and the consumers play under capitalism, he
could not see the difference between freedom
and slavery. Because in his eyes the workers
were only workers and not also customers, he
believed they were already slaves under capitalism, and that one did not change their status when nationalizing all plants and shops.
Socialism substitutes the sovereignty of a dictator, or committee of dictators, for the sovereignty of the consumers. Along with the economic sovereignty of the citizens disappears
also their political sovereignty. To the unique
production plan that annuls any planning on
the part of the consumers corresponds in the
constitutional sphere the one party principle
that deprives the citizens of any opportunity
to plan the course of public affairs. Freedom

is indivisible. He who has not the faculty to choose among various brands of canned food or soap, is also deprived of the power to choose between various political parties and programs and to elect the officeholders. He is no longer a man; he becomes a pawn in the hands of the supreme social engineer. Even his freedom to rear progeny will be taken away by eugenics. Of course, the socialist leaders occasionally assure us that dictatorial tyranny is to last only for the period of transition from capitalism and representative government to the socialist millennium in which everybody's wants and wishes will be fully satisfied.[3] Once the socialist regime is "sufficiently secure to risk criticism," Miss Joan Robinson, the eminent representative of the British neo-Cambridge school, is kind enough to promise us, "even independent philharmonic societies" will be allowed to

[3] Karl Marx, *Sur Kritik des Sozialdemoskratischen Programms von Gotha*, ed. Kreibich (Reichenberg, 1920), p. 23.

exist.[4] Thus the liquidation of all dissenters is the condition that will bring us what the communists call freedom. From this point of view we may also understand what another distinguished Englishman, Mr. J.G. Crowther, had in mind when he praised inquisition as "beneficial to science when it protects a rising class."[5] The meaning of all this is clear. When all people meekly bow to a dictator, there will no longer be any dissenters left for liquidation. Caligula, Torquemada, Robespierre would have agreed with this solution.

The socialists have engineered a semantic revolution in converting the meaning of terms into their opposite. In the vocabulary of their "Newspeak," as George Orwell called it, there is a term "the one-party principle." Now etymologically party is derived from the noun part. The brotherless part is no longer

---

[4] Joan Robinson, *Private Enterprise and Public Control* (published for the Association for Education in Citzenship by the English Universities Press, Ltd., s.d.), pp. 13–14.

[5] J.G. Crowther, *Social Relations of Science* (London, 1941), p. 333.

different from its antonym, the whole; it is identical with it. A brotherless party is not a party, and the one party principle is in fact a no-party principle. It is a suppression of any kind of opposition. Freedom implies the right to choose between assent and dissent. But in Newspeak it means the duty to assent unconditionally and strict interdiction of dissent. This reversal of the traditional connotation of all words of the political terminology is not merely a peculiarity of the language of the Russian Communists and their Fascist and Nazi disciples. The social order that in abolishing private property deprives the consumers of their autonomy and independence, and thereby subjects every man to the arbitrary discretion of the central planning board, could not win the support of the masses if they were not to camouflage its main character. The socialists would have never duped the voters if they had openly told them that their ultimate end is to cast them into bondage. For exoteric use they were forced to pay lip-service to the traditional appreciation of liberty.

IV

I T WAS DIFFERENT in the esoteric discussions among the inner circles of the great conspiracy. There the initiated did not dissemble their intentions concerning liberty. Liberty was, in their opinion, certainly a good feature in the past in the frame of bourgeois society because it provided them with the opportunity to embark on their schemes. But once socialism has triumphed, there is no longer any need for free thought and autonomous action on the part of individuals. Any further change can only be a deviation from the perfect state that mankind has attained in reaching the bliss of socialism. Under such conditions, it would be simply lunacy to tolerate dissent.

Liberty, says the Bolshevist, is a bourgeois prejudice. The common man does not have any ideas of his own, he does not write books, does not hatch heresies, and does not invent new methods of production. He just wants to enjoy life. He has no use for the class interests of the intellectuals who make a living as professional dissenters and innovators.

This is certainly the most arrogant disdain of the plain citizen ever devised. There is no need to argue this point. For the question is not whether or not the common man can himself take advantage of the liberty to think, to speak, and to write books. The question is whether or not the sluggish routinist profits from the freedom granted to those who eclipse him in intelligence and will power. The common man may look with indifference and even contempt upon the dealings of better people. But he is delighted to enjoy all the benefits which the endeavors of the innovators put at his disposal. He has no comprehension of what in his eyes is merely inane hair-splitting. But as soon as these thoughts and theories are utilized by enterprising businessmen for satisfying some of his latent wishes, he hurries to acquire the new products. The common man is without doubt the main beneficiary of all the accomplishments of modern science and technology.

It is true, a man of average intellectual abilities has no chance to rise to the rank of a captain of industry. But the sovereignty that the market assigns to him in economic affairs stimulates technologists and promoters to convert to his use all the achievements of scientific research. Only people whose intellectual horizon does not extend beyond the internal organization of the factory and who do not realize what makes the businessmen run, fail to notice this fact.

The admirers of the Soviet system tell us again and again that freedom is not the supreme good. It is "not worth having," if it implies poverty. To sacrifice it in order to attain wealth for the masses, is in their eyes fully justified. But for a few unruly individualists who cannot adjust themselves to the ways of regular fellows, all people in Russia are perfectly happy. We may leave it undecided whether this happiness was also shared by the millions of Ukrainian peasants who died from starvation, by the inmates of the forced labor camps, and by the Marxian leaders who were purged. But we cannot pass over the fact that the standard of living was incomparably higher in the free countries of the West than in the communist East. In giving away liberty as the price to be paid for the acquisition of prosperity, the Russians made a poor bargain. They now have neither the one nor the other.

V

ROMANTIC philosophy labored under the illusion that in the early ages of history the individual was free and that the course of historical evolution deprived him of his primordial liberty. As Jean Jacques Rousseau saw it, nature accorded men freedom and society enslaved him. In fact, primeval man was at the mercy of every fellow who was stronger and therefore could snatch away from him the scarce means of subsistence. There is in nature nothing to which the name of liberty could be given. The concept of freedom always refers to social relations between men. True, society cannot realize the illusory concept of the individual's absolute independence. Within society everyone depends on what other people are prepared to contribute to his well-being in return for his own contribution to their well-being. Society is essentially the mutual exchange of services. As far as individuals have the opportunity to choose, they are free; if they are forced by violence or threat of violence to surrender to the terms of an exchange, no matter how they feel about it, they lack freedom. This slave is unfree precisely because the master assigns him his tasks and determines what he has to receive if he fulfills it.

As regards the social apparatus of repression and coercion, the government, there cannot be any question of freedom. Government is essentially the negation of liberty. It is the recourse to violence or threat of violence in order to make all people obey the orders of the government, whether they like it or not. As far as the government's jurisdiction extends, there is coercion, not freedom. Government is a necessary institution, the means to make the social system of cooperation work smoothly without being disturbed by violent acts on the part of gangsters whether of domestic or of foreign origin. Government is not, as some people like to say, a necessary evil; it is not an evil, but a means, the only means available to make peaceful human coexistence possible. But it is the opposite of liberty. It is beating, imprisoning, hanging. Whatever a government does it is ultimately supported by the actions of armed constables. If the government operates a school or a hospital, the funds required are collected by taxes, i.e., by payments exacted from the citizens.

If we take into account the fact that, as human nature is, there can neither be civilization nor peace without the functioning of the government apparatus of violent action, we may call government the most beneficial human institution. But the fact remains that government is repression not freedom. Freedom is to be found only in the sphere in which government does not interfere. Liberty is always freedom from the government. It is the restriction of the government's interference. It prevails only in the fields in which the citizens have the opportunity to choose the way in which they want to proceed. Civil rights are the statutes that precisely circumscribe the sphere in which the men conducting the affairs of state are permitted to restrict the individuals' freedom to act.

The ultimate end that men aim at by establishing government is to make possible the operation of a definite system of social cooperation under the principle of the division of labor. If the social system which people want to have is socialism (communism, planning) there is no sphere of freedom left. All citizens are in every regard subject to orders of the government. The state is a total state; the regime is totalitarian. The government alone plans and forces everybody to behave according with this unique plan. In the market economy the individuals are free to choose the way in which they want to integrate themselves into the frame of social cooperation. As far as the sphere of market exchange extends, there is spontaneous action on the part of individuals. Under this system that is called laissez-faire, and which Ferdinand Lassalle dubbed as the night-watchman state, there is freedom because there is a field in which individuals are free to plan for themselves.

The socialists must admit there cannot be any freedom under a socialist system. But they try to obliterate the difference between the servile state and economic freedom by denying that there is any freedom in the mutual exchange of commodities and services on the market. Every market exchange is, in the words of a school of pro-socialist lawyers, "a coercion over other people's liberty." There is, in their eyes, no difference worth mentioning between a man's paying a tax or a fine imposed by a magistrate, or his buying a newspaper or admission to a movie. In each of these cases the man is subject to governing power. He's not free, for, as professor Hale says, a man's freedom means "the absence of any obstacle to his use of material goods."[6] This means: I am not free, because a woman who has knitted a sweater, perhaps as a birthday present for her husband, puts an obstacle to my using it. I myself am restricting all other people's freedom because I object to their using my toothbrush. In doing this I am, according to this doctrine, exercising private governing power, which is analogous to public government power, the powers that the government exercises in imprisoning a man in Sing Sing.

Those expounding this amazing doctrine consistently conclude that liberty is nowhere to be found. They assert that what they call economic pressures do not essentially differ from the pressures the masters practice with regard to their slaves. They reject what they call private governmental power, but they don't object to the restriction of liberty by public government power. They want to concentrate all what

---

[6]   Robert L. Hale, *Freedom Through Law, Public Control of Private Governing Power* (New York: Columbia University, 1952), pp. 4 ff.

they call restrictions of liberty in the hands of the government. They attack the institution of private property and the laws that, as they say, stand "ready to enforce property rights—that is, to deny liberty to anyone to act in a way which violates them."[7]

A generation ago all housewives prepared soup by proceeding in accordance with the recipes that they had got from their mothers or from a cookbook. Today many housewives prefer to buy a canned soup, to warm it and to serve it to their family. But, say our learned doctors, the canning corporation is in a position to restrict the housewife's freedom because, in asking a price for the tin can, it puts an obstacle to her use of it. People who did not enjoy the privilege of being tutored by these eminent teachers, would say that the canned product was turned out by the cannery, and that the corporation in producing it removed the greatest obstacle to a consumer's getting and using a can,

---

[7] Ibid., p. 5.

viz., its nonexistence. The mere essence of a product cannot gratify anybody without its existence. But they are wrong, say the doctors. The corporation dominates the housewife, it destroys by its excessive concentrated power over her individual freedom, and it is the duty of the government to prevent such a gross offense. Corporations, say, under the auspices of the Ford Foundation, another of this group, Professor Berle, must be subjected to the control of the government.[8]

Why does our housewife buy the canned product rather than cling to the methods of her mother and grandmother? No doubt because she thinks this way of acting is more advantageous for her than the traditional custom. Nobody forced her. There were people—they are called jobbers, promoters, capitalists, speculators, stock exchange gamblers—who had the idea of satisfying a latent wish of millions of housewives by investing

---

[8] A.A. Berle, Jr., *Economic Power and the Free Society, a Preliminary Discussion of the Corporation* (New York: The Fund for the Republic, 1954).

in the cannery industry. And there are other equally selfish capitalists who, in many hundreds of other corporations, provide consumers with many hundreds of other things. The better a corporation serves the public, the more customers it gets, the bigger it grows. Go into the home of the average American family and you will see for whom the wheels of the machines are turning.

In a free country nobody is prevented from acquiring riches by serving the consumers better than they are served already. What he needs is only brains and hard work. "Modern civilization, nearly all civilization," said Edwin Cannan, the last in a long line of eminent British economists, "is based on the principle of making things pleasant for those who please the market, and unpleasant for those who fail to do so."[9] All this talk about the concentration of economic power is vain. The bigger a corporation is, the more

---

[9] Edwin Cannan, *An Economist's Protest* (London, 1928), pp. VI ff.

people it serves, the more does it depend on pleasing the consumers, the many, the masses. Economic power, in the market economy, is in the hands of the consumers.

Capitalistic business is not perseverance in the once attained state of production. It is rather ceaseless innovation, daily repeated attempts to improve the provision of the consumers by new, better and cheaper products. Any actual state of production activities is merely transitory. There prevails incessantly the tendency to supplant what is already achieved by something that serves the consumers better. There is consequently under capitalism a continuous circulation of elites. What characterizes the men whom one calls the captains of industry is the ability to contribute new ideas and to put them to work. However big a corporation must be, it is doomed as soon as it does not succeed in adjusting itself daily anew to the best possible methods of serving the consumers. But the politicians and other would-be reformers see only the structure of industry as its exists today. They think that they are cleverer enough to snatch from business control of the plants as they are today, and to manage them by sticking to already established routines. While the ambitious newcomer, who will be the tycoon of tomorrow, is already preparing plans for things unheard of before, all they have in mind is to conduct affairs along tracks already beaten. There is no record of an industrial innovation contrived and put into practice by bureaucrats. If one does not want to plunge into stagnation, a free hand must be left to those today unknown men who have the ingenuity to lead mankind forward on the way to more and more satisfactory conditions. This is the main problem of a nation's economic organization.

Private property of the material factors of production is not a restriction of the freedom of all other people to choose what suits them best. It is, on the contrary, the means that assigns to the common man, in his capacity as a buyer, supremacy in all economic affairs. It is the means to stimulate a nation's most enterprising men to exert themselves to the best of their abilities in the service of all of the people.

VI

HOWEVER, one does not exhaustively describe the sweeping changes that capitalism brought about in the conditions of the common man if one merely deals with the supremacy he enjoys on the market as a consumer and in the affairs of state as a voter and with the unprecedented improvement of his standard of living. No less important is the fact that capitalism has made it possible for him to save, to accumulate capital and to invest it. The gulf that in the pre-capitalistic status and caste society separated the owners of property from the penniless poor has been narrowed down. In older ages the journeyman had such a low pay that he could hardly lay by something and, if he nevertheless did so, he could only keep his savings by hoarding and hiding a

few coins. Under capitalism his competence makes saving possible, and there are
institutions that enable him to invest his
funds in business. A not inconsiderable
amount of the capital employed in American industries is the counterpart of the savings of employees. In acquiring savings
deposits, insurance policies, bonds and also
common stock, wage earners and salaried
people are themselves earning interest and
dividends and thereby, in the terminology
of Marxism, are exploiters. The common
man is directly interested in the flowering
of business not only as a consumer and as
an employee, but also as an investor. There
prevails a tendency to efface to some extent
the once sharp difference between those
who own factors of production and those
who do not. But, of course, this trend can
only develop where the market economy is
not sabotaged by allegedly social policies.
The welfare state with its methods of easy
money, credit expansion and undisguised
inflation continually takes bites out of all
claims payable in units of the nation's legal

tender. The self-styled champions of the common man are still guided by the obsolete idea that a policy that favors the debtors at the expense of the creditors is very beneficial to the majority of the people. Their inability to comprehend the essential characteristics of the market economy manifests itself also in their failure to see the obvious fact that those whom they feign to aid are creditors in their capacity as savers, policy holders, and owners of bonds.

VII

THE DISTINCTIVE principle of Western social philosophy is individualism. It aims at the creation of a sphere in which the individual is free to think, to choose, and to act without being restrained by the interference of the social apparatus of coercion and oppression, the State. All the spiritual and material achievements of Western civilization were the result of the operation of this idea of liberty.

This doctrine and the policies of individualism and of capitalism, its application to economic matters, do not need any apologists or propagandists. The achievements speak for themselves.

The case for capitalism and private property rests, apart from other considerations, also upon the incomparable efficiency of its productive effort. It is this efficiency that makes it possible for capitalistic business to support a rapidly increasing population at a continually improving standard of living. The resulting progressive prosperity of the masses creates a social environment in which the exceptionally gifted individuals are free to give to their fellow-citizens all they are able to give. The social system of private property and limited government is the only system that tends to debarbarize all those who have the innate capacity to acquire personal culture.

It is a gratuitous pastime to belittle the material achievements of capitalism by observing that there are things that are more essential for mankind than bigger and speedier motorcars, and homes equipped with central heating, air conditioning, refrigerators, washing machines, and television sets. There certainly are such higher and nobler pursuits. But they are higher and nobler precisely because they cannot be aspired to by any external effort, but require the individual's personal determination and exertion. Those levelling this reproach against capitalism display a rather crude and materialistic view in assuming that moral and spiritual culture could be built either by the government or by the organization of production activities. All that these external factors can achieve in this regard is to bring about an environment and a competence which offers the individuals the opportunity to work at their own personal perfection and edification. It is not the fault of capitalism that the masses prefer a boxing match to a performance of Sophocles' *Antigone*, jazz music to Beethoven symphonies, and comics to poetry. But it is certain that while pre-capitalistic conditions as they still prevail in the much greater part of the world makes these good things accessible only to a small minority of people, capitalism gives to the many a favorable chance of striving after them.

From whatever angle one may look at capitalism there is no reason to lament the passing of the allegedly good old days. Still less is it justified to long for the totalitarian utopias, whether of the Nazi or of the Soviet type.

We are inaugurating tonight the ninth meeting of the Mont Pelerin Society. It is fitting to remember on this occasion that meetings of this kind in which opinions opposed to those of the majority of our contemporaries and to those of their governments are advanced and are possible only in the climate of liberty and freedom that is the most precious mark of Western civilization. Let us hope that this right to dissent will never disappear.

Manufactured by Amazon.ca
Bolton, ON